A FRIEND IN THE LIBRARY

RELIGION

BY

EVA MARCH TAPPAN

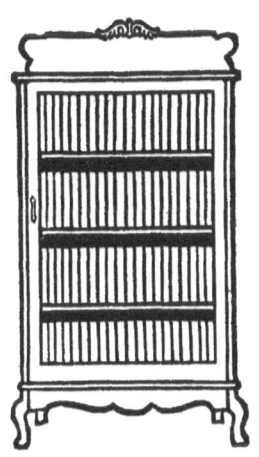

British Library Cataloguing-in-Publication Data
A catalogue record for this book is available from the
British Library

RELIGION

A FRIEND IN THE LIBRARY

A Practical Guide to the Writings of

RALPH WALDO EMERSON

NATHANIEL HAWTHORNE

HENRY WADSWORTH LONGFELLOW

JAMES RUSSELL LOWELL

JOHN GREENLEAF WHITTIER

OLIVER WENDELL HOLMES

IN TWELVE VOLUMES

VOLUME VIII

Eva March Tappan

Eva March Tappan was born on 26th December 1854 in Blackstone, Massachusetts, America. She is well known as a factual as well as fictional writer, but spent her early career as a teacher. Tappan was the only child of Reverend Edmund March Tappan and Lucretia Logée, and received her education at the esteemed Vassar College. This was a private coeducational liberal arts college, in the town of Poughkeepsie, New York, from which she graduated in 1875. Here, Tappan was a member of Phi Beta Kappa, the oldest honour society for the liberal arts and sciences, widely considered as the nations most prestigious society. She also edited the *Vassar Miscellany,* a college publication.

After leaving her early education, Tappan began teaching at Wheaton College, one of the oldest institutions of higher education for women in the United States, founded in 1834 and based in Norton, Massachusetts. She taught Latin and German here, from 1875 until 1880, before moving on to the Raymond Academy in Camden, New Jersey where she was associate Principal until 1894. Tappan also received a graduate degree in English Literature from the University of Pennsylvania. This allowed her to pursue her first love, that of reading and writing, and she taught as head of the English department at the English High School at Worcester, Massachusetts.

It was only after this date that Tappan began her literary career, writing about famous characters in history, often aimed at educating children in important historical themes and epochs. Some of her better known works include, *In the Days of William the Conqueror* (1901) and *In the Days of Queen Elizabeth* (1902), *The Out-of-Door Book* (1907), *When Knights Were Bold* (1911) and *The Little Book of the Flag* (1917). Tappan never married, being a happy singleton, and died on 29th January 1930, aged seventy-five.

RELIGION

In a little home hidden away among the mountains, a quiet, strong, thinking woman lived. Happiness had come into her life, and also sorrow; but she had looked up to the hills and had found strength. One day she spoke, gently and almost with an apology, of some of the hard things that she had had to meet. Then she said half shyly, "I will show you what has helped me. I call it *my* poem." She brought from an inner room a scrap-book. Bookstores were a long way off, and this was a home-made book. Its leaves were of wrapping paper, each leaf made of two or three folds glued together for strength and stiffness. Here were pasted many poems and bits of prose cut from the newspapers, every one of real merit and of some literary value. The book fell open of itself, and on the page before us was Whittier's "The Eternal Goodness" (ii. 267). She pointed out her favorite stanzas. One was: —

> I long for household voices gone,
>> For vanished smiles I long;
> But God hath led my dear ones on,
>> And He can do no wrong.

Another was: —

> I know not what the future hath
>> Of marvel or surprise,
> Assured alone that life and death
>> His mercy underlies.

And, last: —

> I know not where His islands lift
>> Their fronded palms in air;
> I only know I cannot drift
>> Beyond His love and care.

She closed the simple, home-made book, and began to speak of other things: of the sunset light on the ripening apples, of the little river which we could hear rippling over the stones, of whether rain would fall on the morrow. When I saw the little book again, it had become a tenderly loved relic. We touched it gently and reverently. Just beyond "The Eternal Goodness," another poem had been added. It was "Our Master" (Whittier, ii. 272), and around one stanza a line had been drawn: —

> To do Thy will is more than praise,
>   As words are less than deeds;
> And simple trust can find Thy ways
>   We miss with chart of creeds.

So it was that Whittier had brought comfort and help to the little home in the shadow of the mountains.

A FRIEND IN THE LIBRARY

Whittier's religious poems are full of questioning, of eagerness to know what is beyond, and the meaning of what is in sight. He says ("Questions of Life," ii. 236) : —

> I am: how little more I know!
> Whence came I? Whither do I go?
> A centred self, which feels and is;
> A cry between the silences.

So he ponders, sometimes

> O'erburdened with a sense
> Of life, and cause, and consequence;

and meditating on

> The same old baffling questions! O my friend,
> I cannot answer them,

he says ("Trust," ii. 242); but he always comes to the glad conclusion (ii. 236), —

> Assured that all I know is best,
> And humbly trusting for the rest.

No one could be further than Whittier from drawing sectarian lines; but on every page of his writings one can trace the Quaker influence. Sometimes it is just a wee bit amusing. The city maiden of "Among the Hills" (i. 260) probably did not wear a silk dress into the hayfield, but the poet speaks of her "silken armor," with all the Quaker dislike of garments that gleam and shine. "Pride" is a thing which he abhors. He forgets that shoes have become a necessity of life, and grieves that the feet of the "Barefoot Boy" must soon be hidden "in the prison-house of pride." Of "fashion" — that is, the fashion of other folk — he has as sincere a horror as so kindly a man can feel; but he forgets that there is as much fashion in the stand-up collar of *his* coat as in the turned-down collars of other folk; and that the ordered silence of the Friends' meeting is in its principle as purely a ritualistic form of worship as the banner-led processional and the altar gleaming with candles. Whittier's quiet defense of the Friends' meeting ("The Meeting," ii. 278) is most beautiful. There is about it all the stillness of the "deeper rest" of the quiet room, the "silence all unbroken," the "words of fitness," the "breath of a diviner air." One of the most perfect of his religious poems is his beautiful litany, "At Last" (ii. 333). He pleads: —

Be near me when all else is from me drifting:
    Earth, sky, home's pictures, days of shade and
        shine,
And kindly faces to my own uplifting
    The love which answers mine.

Whittier declared ("The Meeting," ii. 278) that he asked

> No organ's soulless breath
> To drone the themes of life and death,

but in this poem we can almost feel the throb of the organ music. One can hardly read it, even silently, without unconsciously making it into a chant.

It is such poems as this that refuse to be mere words, however melodious, and carry about them an over-tone of music that, once heard, haunts the mind forever after. One of these is in Longfellow's "Golden Legend" (v. 169), which begins,—

> The night is calm and cloudless,
> And still as still can be,
> And the stars come forth to listen
> To the music of the sea.

This "Golden Legend," and "The Divine Tragedy," which precedes it, are parts of "Christus," a long dramatic poem. The poet's plan was to picture the times of Christ in "The Divine Tragedy," and the Middle Ages in "The Golden Legend." "The New England Tragedies," though not perfectly satisfactory to the author, was used as a third part of the trilogy. In his note-book he suggests that "The Divine Tragedy" should stand for the age of faith, the "Legend" for the age of hope, and the more modern dramas for the age of charity. Many of Longfellow's religious poems have been more general favorites than these. Two of his Christmas poems are loved by all who know them. One is his "Christmas Bells" (iii. 139), beginning,—

RELIGION

> I heard the bells on Christmas Day
> Their old, familiar carols play,
> And wild and sweet
> The words repeat
> Of peace on earth, good will to men!

The poem was written during the Civil War. Of this war he says, —

> It was as if an earthquake rent
> The hearthstones of a continent.

Longfellow's second Christmas poem is his "Three Kings" (iii. 122), the story of the Wise Men who came out of the East to give honor to the Christ-Child. Longfellow's religion is practical, as poems like "Resignation" (i. 303) and others show; but he loves the legends of early ages. One of his "Tales of a Wayside Inn" is such a story of the appearance of Christ to those who are worthy as has

found its best rounded form in the legend of
the Holy Grail. In this "Legend Beautiful"
(iv. 185), the vision of the Christ comes to a
monk. But as he kneels, "wondering, wor-
shiping, adoring," the bell of the convent
rings. The hour had come when

> All the blind and halt and lame,
> All the beggars of the street,

came to the convent portals for the daily bread
which it was his task to distribute among
them. What should he do?

> Deep distress and hesitation
> Mingled with his adoration;
> Should he go or should he stay?
> Should he leave the poor to wait
> Hungry at the convent gate,
> Till the Vision passed away?

Should he slight his radiant guest,
Slight this visitant celestial,
For a crowd of ragged, bestial
Beggars at the convent gate?

So the poor, troubled monk ponders, anxious to do the right, perplexed to find the right. Longfellow leads on the story through the monk's doubt and uncertainty to his final decision and the beautiful ending of the poem. Another legend upon which he founded a poem is from the Talmud. It is of the mighty angel Sandalphon (iii. 60), whose feet rest upon earth and whose head reaches to the door of Heaven. He is one of the three who weave the prayers of the Israelites into garlands and bear them to the throne of God. The loftiness of the theme touched the poet's imagination, and he has written a noble poem which achieves a height and majesty of rare excellence. He tells the story, then he says : —

> It is but a legend, I know,—
> A fable, a phantom, a show,
>   Of the ancient Rabbinical lore;
> Yet the old mediæval tradition,
> The beautiful, strange superstition,
>   But haunts me and holds me the more.
>
> When I look from my window at night,
> And the welkin above is all white,
>   All throbbing and panting with stars,
> Among them majestic is standing
> Sandalphon, the angel, expanding
>   His pinions in nebulous bars.

There is something wonderfully fine about that last stanza. It gives us a glimpse of the richness of the thoughts and dreams that throng into the poet's heart. For an instant we can almost fancy ourselves to be poets; for one golden moment we look at the earth and the heavens through their eyes.

Longfellow's translations are exceedingly good. They are poetical and musical, and also simple and literal. Among his other work of the sort, he translated parts of "Frithiof's Saga" (vi. 219), of the Swedish Bishop Tegnér. Tegnér expressed much pleasure at this and wrote to Longfellow, begging him to complete the work. "After this kind letter," wrote Longfellow to a friend, "can I do less than overset the 'Nattvardsbarnen'?" This was "The Children of the Lord's Supper" (vi. 227). Before reading it, one ought to read Longfellow's charming note (vi. 470), which brings before us the simple village life of Sweden seventy-five years ago as clearly as a picture. Then turn back to the poem and read of the "Pentecost, day of rejoicing," —

When the young, their parents' hope, and the loved
    ones of heaven,
Should at the foot of the altar renew the vows of their
    baptism.

The poem is the beautiful story of the hour in the church. We follow the children as they recite the answers of the catechism to the questioning of the kindly pastor, "the old man of seventy winters."

                And now at the beck of the old man
Knee against knee they knitted a wreath round the
    altar's enclosure.
Kneeling he read then the prayers of the consecration,
    and softly
With him the children read; at the close, with tremu-
    lous accents,
Asked he the peace of heaven, a benediction upon them.

RELIGION

At the end of the service, —

> With heaven in their hearts and their faces,
> Up rose the children all, and each bowed him, weeping
>   full sorely,
> Downward to kiss that reverend hand, but all of them
>   pressed he,
> Moved, to his bosom, and laid, with a prayer, his hands
>   full of blessings,
> Now on the holy breast, and now on the innocent
>   tresses.

In Longfellow's religious poems we rarely, if ever, find the earnestness of inquiry that is so characteristic of Whittier. The Quaker poet asks whence and whither; he reasons and he questions, but always reaches the one end that God is love and one may safely trust in Him for whatever may betide. Longfellow asks no questions, he never suggests doubt.

The tender buds expanding into blossoms are to him ("Flowers," i. 26), —

Emblems of our own great resurrection,
Emblems of the bright and better land.

The refrain of "The Old Clock on the Stairs" (i. 256), "Forever — never!" he interprets as

Never here, forever there,
Where all parting, pain, and care,
And death, and time, shall disappear, —
Forever there, but never here!

In our best writers there is much religious feeling, flowing on in undercurrent, even if not always coming to the surface; but there is little theology and less sectarianism. In the early days of the Civil War Holmes wrote ("Bread and the Newspapers," viii. 1): "When the masked battery opens, does the

'Baptist' Lieutenant believe in his heart that God takes better care of him than of his 'Congregationalist' Colonel?" And at the funeral services of those who have fallen we hear very little, he says, "of the dogmas on which men differ; very much of the faith and trust in which all sincere Christians can agree. It is a noble lesson."

Holmes questions as earnestly as Whittier, and with even more eagerness puts forward the scientist's demand for the exact truth.

Between two breaths what crowded mysteries lie,—
The first short gasp, the last and long-drawn sigh!

So he ponders in his "Rhymed Lesson" (xii. 107). He says: —

Oh, who forgets when first the piercing thought
Through childhood's musings found its way unsought?

A FRIEND IN THE LIBRARY

I AM, — I LIVE. The mystery and the fear
When the dread question, "What has brought me
    here?"
Burst through life's twilight, as before the sun
Roll the deep thunders of the morning gun!

He is interested in the peculiarities and od-
dities of theological lore and custom. He is
not satisfied with surface drift, he is always
probing for bed-rock. One of his suggestions
is that he who is searching for truth should
"depolarize every fixed religious idea in the
mind by changing the word which stands for
it." He says this in "The Professor at the
Breakfast-Table" (ii. 6), and the Divinity
Student asks what he means by "depolariz-
ing." The Professor replies: —

When a given symbol which represents a thought
has lain for a certain length of time in the mind, it
undergoes a change like that which rest in a certain

position gives to iron. It becomes magnetic in its relations, — it is traversed by strange forces which did not belong to it. The word, and consequently the idea it represents, is *polarized*.

The religious currency of mankind, in thought, in speech, and in print, consists entirely of polarized words. Borrow one of these from another language and religion, and you will find it leaves all its magnetism behind it. Take that famous word O'm, of the Hindoo mythology. Even a priest cannot pronounce it without sin; and a holy Pundit would shut his ears and run away from you in horror, if you should say it aloud. What do you care for O'm? If you wanted to get the Pundit to look at his religion fairly, you must first depolarize this and all similar words for him.

So it is that the poet-scientist thinks and reasons and investigates; but in the end he comes to the trustfulness of Whittier, the assurance of Longfellow. He says of people

("Over the Teacups," iv. 40), "Little children
they come from the hands of the Father of all;
little children in their helplessness, their igno-
rance, they are going back to Him." Holmes's
"Sun-Day Hymn" (xii. 430), "Lord of all
being, throned afar," stands in the Episcopal
Hymnal with a hymn by the Methodist
Charles Wesley on one side and one by the
Churchman Bishop Coxe on the other.
Holmes's "Chambered Nautilus" (xii. 393) is
a poem of exact science and close observation
as well as of religion. Only a physician and
poet could have written Holmes's "The Liv-
ing Temple" (xii. 252) with its accurate
physiology and its poetry. In this he says of
the heart: —

> No rest that throbbing slave may ask,
> Forever quivering o'er his task,

RELIGION

While far and wide a crimson jet
Leaps forth to fill the woven net
Which in unnumbered crossing tides
The flood of burning life divides,
Then, kindling each decaying part,
Creeps back to find the throbbing heart.

Emerson's religious thought was marked by the accuracy of the close observer, the reasonableness of the philosopher, the perception of order and method and beauty of the poet. He looked upon every person and every object in nature with a sort of expectant reverence; for that person, however humble, might have caught the sound of some word of God's which had not come to his own ears; the rose or the apple-blossom in his garden might be the visible expression of some thought of God's which had not entered his own mind. In writing of immortality (viii. 321), he says: —

Here are people who cannot dispose of a day; an hour hangs heavy on their hands; and will you offer them rolling ages without end?

Quote this sentence alone, and it appears to be the most irreverent satire; but read his following sentences in all their glorious prophecy: —

Within every man's thought is a higher thought, — within the character he exhibits to-day, a higher character.

This nobler part may develop, he says, the man

entering deeper into God, God into him, until the last garment of egotism falls, and he is with God, — shares the will and the immensity of the First Cause.

RELIGION

There is a story that somebody said to one of those restless mortals who never have time to do anything properly because they are in so great a flurry to get to the next thing, "But if you are going to live forever, why are you in such a hurry?" In like manner, Emerson asks, "Why should I hasten to solve every riddle which life offers me? I am well assured that the Questioner who brings me so many problems will bring the answers also in due time" ("Worship," vi. 199). Emerson is never in a hurry. "It is not my duty to prove to myself the immortality of the soul," he says quietly ("Immortality," viii. 321). Nevertheless, at the beginning of the essay he writes with quiet assurance, if not with mathematical proof: —

What is excellent,

As God lives, is permanent;

Hearts are dust, hearts' loves remain;

Heart's love will meet thee again.

All that I have seen [he says] teaches me to trust the Creator for all I have not seen. Whatever it be which the great Providence prepares for us, it must be something large and generous, and in the great style of his works.

A little further on he reminds us that every really able man feels that his work is not so good as it should be. "What is this Better, this flying ideal," he questions, "but the perpetual promise of his Creator?" This fancy of the "flying Ideal" is brought out in his poem, "Forerunners" (ix. 85).

Emerson was much interested in Swedenborg, and in his "Representative Men" (iv. 91), chose him as "the mystic." He describes him as the practical and original scientist, who "anticipated much science of the nineteenth century." He quotes from Swedenborg's writings his theory of the earth and its meaning, his belief that "if we choose to express any natural truth in physical and definite vocal terms, and to convert these terms only into the corresponding and spiritual terms, we shall by this means elicit a spiritual truth or theological dogma, in place of the physical truth or precept." Then he expresses this idea of correspondence more simply, as follows: "That every sensible object, — animal, rock, river, air, — nay, space and time, subsists not for itself, nor finally to a material end, but as a picture language to tell another story of beings and duties"; that is, "A house signifies carnal understanding; a tree, perception; the moon, faith." Emerson objects to this interpretation of nature as being "mystical and Hebraic" rather than "human and universal"; but Emerson, too, believed in nature as expressing God's thoughts; and, however widely varying ideas of details the two men might form, he could not help looking with a warm admiration upon the services which Swedenborg rendered to the world in the joy and worship aroused in him by the harmonies which he perceived.

Not every one is able to read Swedenborg's many volumes, and not every one would care to follow out his symbolism; but Emerson's essay on "Demonology" (x. 1) is based largely on experiences which everybody has had in greater or less degree. In demonology he includes dreams, signs, omens, and belief in luck. In another essay ("Worship," vi. 199) he declares that "Shallow men believe in luck"; and here he says that these things "deserve notice chiefly because every man has usually in a lifetime two or three hints in this kind which are specially impressive to him. Most people have a bit of superstition lurking in some dark corner of their minds; and most people scorn the superstitions of others. 'I have no respect for any one who believes in signs,' declared a lady with emphasis, 'but of course if a bird flies into a window, it is almost a sure sign of death.'"

Like all of Emerson's essays, this one is full of new ideas and suggestions. He speaks of the strange power which carries two sleeping children locked in each other's arms to distant parts of the world and far removed from each other; of the common feeling that the experience which one is passing through he has met before; of the possible significance of the human look in the eyes of a dog; of the prophecies of dreams and the occasional revelation of characteristics in them; of "lucky" days and persons, "as if," he says, "the laws of the Father of the universe were sometimes balked and eluded by a meddlesome Aunt of the universe for her pets."

Emerson finds more than one lesson in this subject, but one of the best is closely connected in thought with his essay on "Compensation" (ii. 91). He says, "The history of man is a series of conspiracies to win from Nature some advantage without paying for it"; and he closes with the thought: —

The whole world is an omen and a sign. Why look so wistfully in a corner? Man is the image of

God. Why run after a ghost or a dream? The voice of divination resounds everywhere and runs to waste unheard, unregarded, as the mountains echo with the bleatings of cattle.

In Emerson's "Representative Men" (iv.) he chooses Plato for the ideal philosopher. Of him he speaks with such enthusiastic appreciation that even a few extracts from his essay give a better idea of it than the most careful summary. Here are some of his words: —

Out of Plato come all things that are still written and debated among men of thought.

An Englishman reads Plato and says, "how English!" a German, "how Teutonic!" an Italian, "how Roman and how Greek!"

He [Plato] has finished his thinking before he brings it to the reader.

Plato affirms the coincidence of science and virtue; for vice can never know itself and virtue, but virtue knows both itself and vice. The eye attested that justice was best, as long as it was profitable; Plato affirms that it is profitable throughout; that the profit is intrinsic, though the just conceal his justice from gods and men; that it is better to suffer injustice than to do it; that the sinner ought to covet punishment; that the lie was more hurtful than homicide; . . . that the order or proceeding of nature was from the mind to the body, and, though a sound body cannot restore an unsound mind, yet a good soul can, by its virtue, render the body the best possible. . . . The fine which the good, refusing to govern, ought to pay, is to be governed by a worse man.

When a man writes a biography of another, he can hardly help noting particularly those points in his hero's character which are in accordance with his own ways of thinking. Of Plato Emerson says, "The secret of his popular success is the moral aim which endeared him to mankind. 'Intellect,' he declares, 'is king of heaven and of earth,' but in Plato, intellect is always moral." So it is with Emerson himself; he appreciates and honors intellect, but with him, as with Plato, "intellect is always moral." For intellect turned aside from its rightful use, he has no respect; it must always lead the way to the moral, to the upright, to the truth which is higher and of finer strain than itself.

ADDITIONAL

Holmes

The Breakfast-Table Series, i., ii., iii., as well as *Pages from an Old Volume of Life* (viii.), are full of keen observations on life, morals, and religion.

Lowell

Longing, ix. 255.
The Cathedral, xiii. 41.
Witchcraft, iii. 113.

Whittier

St. Gregory's Guest, i. 405.
The River Path, ii. 53.
Raphael, ii. 98.
My Triumph, ii. 159.
My Soul and I, ii. 220.
The Shadow and the Light, ii. 252.
Andrew Ryckman's Prayer, ii. 258.
The Two Angels, ii. 309.
On a Sun-Dial, ii. 322.
The Minister's Daughter, ii. 323.

RELIGION

EMERSON

The Lord's Supper, xi. 1.
Religion in England, v. 213.
Remarks at the Free Religious Association, xi. 475.
Speech at the Free Religious Association, xi. 483.

LONGFELLOW

God's Acre, i. 78.
Blind Bartimeus, i. 82.
The Ladder of St. Augustine, iii. 16.
The Sermon of St. Francis, iii. 95.
To-morrow, iii. 146.
Nature, iii. 327.
The Two Rivers, iii. 234.
Auf Wiedersehen, iii. 311.

QUESTIONS

1. Why are the religious writings of our best poets of so much practical value?

   Because there is in them so much religion, both of sentiment and of practice, and so little theology.

2. What are the characteristics of Whittier's religious poems?
    Earnest thought and questioning.

3. What is his invariable conclusion?
    A childlike trust that all is well.

4. How are Whittier's poems marked by the Quaker influence?
    In his reference to "fashion" and "pride" and "forms" of worship.

5. Which poem of Whittier's describes and defends the Friends' meeting?
    The Meeting (ii. 278).

6. Which of Whittier's poems has a marked chant-like quality?
    "At Last" (ii. 333).

7. What was Longfellow's plan for "Christus" (v. 19)?
    That " The Divine Tragedy" should stand for the times of Christ, the age of faith; " The Golden Legend " for the Middle

*Ages, the age of hope;.and " The New
England Tragedies " for modern times,
the age of charity.*

8. What are Longfellow's Christmas poems?
   Christmas Bells (iii. 139), *and The Three
   Kings* (iii. 122).

9. Which is Longfellow's finest poem of religious legend?
   " Sandalphon " (iii. 60).

10. What are the characteristics of Longfellow's
    translations?
    *They are poetical and musical, and also
    simple and literal.*

11. From what languages has he translated?
    *French, German, Swedish, Spanish, Ital-
    ian, Danish, Anglo-Saxon, Portuguese,
    and Latin; and he has also put into
    verse some prose translations from
    Armenian and Persian.*

12. From what is "The Children of the Lord's Supper" (vi. 228) taken?

    From the Swedish of Bishop Tegnêr.

13. How does the religious element of Longfellow's poems compare with that of Whittier's?

    Whittier thinks and ponders and questions, then trusts; Longfellow asks no questions, never suggests doubt or inquiry.

14. How does Holmes treat sectarianism?

    With kindly humor.

15. How does he show himself a scientist even in his religious writings?

    By his scientific accuracy, his keenness, and his demand for the exact truth.

16. What poems of his show these characteristics most clearly?

    The "Chambered Nautilus" (xii. 393) and "The Living Temple" (xii. 252).

17. Why did Emerson look with expectant reverence upon persons and objects in nature?

Because he believed that the person might have caught some word of God which he had not; and the object might symbolize some thought of God which had not been revealed to him.

18. Why do separate sentences quoted from Emerson often give a false idea of his thought?

Because they need the context.

19. What are the characteristics of Emerson's religious thought?

Sincerity, quietness, and a feeling that it is not necessary to "prove all things" in one day.

20. To what general conclusion in religious matters does he come?

"All that I have seen teaches me to trust the Creator for all I have not seen."

21. In what are he and Swedenborg in sympathy?

    In the belief that nature is an expression of the thought of God.

22. Why do so many of Emerson's essays make so wide an appeal?

    Because they are based upon experiences common to all in greater or less degree.

23. In what main point are Plato and Emerson alike?

    In their writings, intellect is always moral.